English
Language
Teacher
Development
Series

Cooperative Learning and Teaching

**GEORGE M. JACOBS
AND HARUMI KIMURA**

Second Edition

Thomas S. C. Farrell, *Series Editor*

 **tesol press**

bookstore.tesol.org

TESOL International Association
1925 Ballenger Avenue, Ste. 550
Alexandria, VA 22314 USA
www.tesol.org

Managing Editor: Tomiko Breland
Copy Editor: Suzy Richardt
Cover and Interior Design: Kathleen Dyson
Head of Education & Events: Sarah Sahr

Recommended citation:
Jacobs, G. M., & Kimura, H. (2023). *Cooperative learning and teaching* (2nd ed.). TESOL International Association.

ISBN 978-1-953745-34-7
ISBN (ebook) 978-1-953745-35-4
Library of Congress Control Number 2023944110

Contents

Series Editor's Preface

The English Language Teacher Development (ELTD) series consists of a set of short resource books for English language teachers that are written in a jargon-free and accessible manner for all types of teachers of English, including experienced and novice teachers. The ELTD series is designed to offer teachers a theory-to-practice approach to English language teaching, and each book offers a wide variety of practical teaching approaches and methods for the topic at hand. Each book also offers opportunities for teachers to interact with the materials presented. The books can be used in preservice settings or in-service courses and by individuals looking for ways to refresh their practice.

The second edition of George M. Jacobs and Harumi Kimura's book, *Cooperative Learning and Teaching,* explores different approaches to cooperative learning and teaching in the English language classroom. This book provides an updated and comprehensive overview of cooperative learning techniques and the teaching of cooperative learning in an easy-to-follow guide that language teachers will find very practical for their own contexts. Topics covered include group work, preparing for cooperative learning, and principles for interaction and bonding in the English language classroom. Four new chapters in this updated edition introduce teachers to the role of positive psychology in cooperative learning, ways to promote interaction in virtual classrooms, connecting cooperative learning to the United Nations' Sustainable Development Goals, and improving cooperation among teachers. *Cooperative Learning and Teaching, Second Edition,* is a valuable addition to the literature in our profession.

I am very grateful to the authors of the ELTD series for sharing their knowledge and expertise with other English language teaching professionals to make these short books affordable for all language teachers throughout the world. It is truly an honor for me to work again with each of these authors for the advancement of English language teaching.

Thomas S. C. Farrell

CHAPTER 1

Introduction

Put simply, cooperative learning (CL) represents a diverse, growing body of ideas for helping students work together effectively and happily. Put even more simply, CL means group activities done with thought. This approach combines a body of literature with each teacher's and each class's own experiences of, reflections on, and beliefs about what constitutes good education. In contrast to CL, group activities may sometimes take place without any forethought. Such impromptu group activities sometimes work well, but our experience suggests that forethought brings rewards. The literature from CL and related areas provides tools for action and reflection, which help teachers increase the chances that students' group activities will be fruitful.

In Chapter 2, "Why Use Group Activities?" we provide background on potential advantages of group activities as well as a frank admission of problems that may arise when students work in groups. The chapter has two goals: (1) to whet readers' appetites for using group activities because of the positive effects that student–student interaction can have and (2) to warn readers that the potential feast of learning and enthusiasm offered by group activities must be prepared with care, because obstacles await between planning and enacting lessons.

Chapter 3, "Preparing for Cooperative Learning," looks at what needs to be considered before the group activities begin. Just as dinner hosts must consider how to arrange the chairs and which guests should sit together, so too must issues of seating be considered when students come together.

Chapter 4, "Four Teaching Principles for Interaction," presents four principles that seek to provide the core energy and direction for CL:

1. *Maximum peer interactions*: How many student–student interactions are taking place and how well are students interacting with their peers?

2. *Equal opportunity to participate*: Do all group members have many chances to share in what the group discusses and does?

3. *Individual accountability*: Do all group members use those chances to share with their group mates?

4. *Positive interdependence*: Do group members feel they are all part of a team and that the learning of everyone on that team represents a crucial purpose of that team?

Chapter 5, "Four Teaching Principles for Bonding," presents four principles aimed to keep groups together and encourage members to reach out to others beyond their small group:

1. *Group autonomy*: Does being in a group help students become less dependent on teachers?

2. *Heterogeneous grouping*: Do groups usually represent a mix of students similar to the mix of students in the whole class?

3. *Cooperation as a value*: Does students' circle of concern extend beyond their small group?

4. *Using cooperative skills*: Does the class know and use skills that help people work together?

Chapter 6, "Cooperative Learning and Positive Psychology," looks at how CL principles fit well with a relatively new approach to psychology, known as positive psychology. Its concepts are highlighted in the acronym PERMA: positive emotion, engagement, relationships, meaning, and accomplishment.

Chapter 7, "Student–Student Interaction in Virtual Classrooms," addresses how CL can be used in online learning. The chapter also looks at the many possible benefits of virtual learning. These benefits mean that virtual classmates will remain an integral part of the future of learning, regardless of pandemics.

Chapter 8, "Cooperative Learning and the United Nations' Sustainable Development Goals," focuses on the CL principle of *cooperation as a value*, the principle that seeks to extend cooperation beyond small classroom groups of two, three, or four members and promote the attitude of "we're all in it together" on a global basis. A related attitude encourages students to see education not just as a tool for their personal and family advancement, but also as a tool to advance the progress of society.

Chapter 9, "Cooperation Among Teachers," may be the book's most important chapter. When teachers see the benefits of cooperation among their own peers, they may become more likely to encourage their students to also engage in peer cooperation. Furthermore, when teachers reflect on how to overcome difficulties in their own peer interactions, they gain insights and empathy into the difficulties their students face in CL.

CHAPTER 2

Why Use Group Activities?

This chapter explores why teachers facilitate group activities and then turns to problems that can arise. By the end of the chapter, you will be able to explain potential advantages of using group activities in your English language classes, and you will have considered ways to address potential difficulties.

Why Use Groups?

In any class, instruction can take place in one of three ways—often, the three ways are combined during the same lesson. Students can listen to the teachers and watch whatever they might be doing (e.g., leading the class to create a piece of writing) or showing (e.g., a video or app), interact with each other in groups, or work alone.

In this book, we urge you to include more small-group (2–4 members) activities in your teaching. Humans participate in group activities all the time in and out of education. Indeed, in the modern world, life would be unthinkable without interacting with fellow humans (Tomasello, 2009).

REFLECTIVE BREAK

- What is a positive experience you have had working with other people?

- What were you doing?

- Why was the experience positive?

Example: *Playing badminton with a friend tested each other's skill and stamina, and we praised each other for hitting good shots.*

Indeed, many advantages potentially arise when English language students work with their peers. Following are some possible benefits:

- Students use the target language more (Ellis, 2012). Producing spoken and written output by talking and writing may boost students' accuracy, fluency, and confidence.

- Students hear and read more understandable instances of the target language (Ellis, 2012). Why? Because peers may speak and write more understandably, and students can help each other with comprehension difficulties they have when listening or reading.

- Students receive more individual attention. One teacher cannot provide much one-on-one help to students, but students' group mates are right there to check their answers and to help with their problems (McCafferty et al., 2006).

- Students' motivation to learn increases because they are learning not only for themselves but also to support their group. If they are not in class, their group mates miss them and encourage them to attend class. Just as individual students support their group, groups provide a support network for the group members (Dornyei, 2020).

- Students learn how to work with others. Such collaborative skills are instrumental in many areas of life, including in the work world (Gillies, 2019).

- Students become less dependent on teachers because peers provide each other with support. Teachers are still there to help, but peers form the first option (Benson, 2011).

- Students get to work with people different from themselves. For instance, students from different countries, religions, ethnic groups, sexual orientations, and socioeconomic levels can form friendships as they work together toward a common goal (Allport, 1954).

- Students enjoy learning more. Humans are social animals (Tomasello, 2009). People usually enjoy doing activities with others; however, in some English language classrooms, the rules have been "eyes on your own paper" and "no talking to your neighbor." Groups make learning a social activity and, thus, more motivating.

- Group activities democratize the classroom. As individuals, students have less power to influence decisions, such as what to study and how to study; in groups, students have more power (Jacobs & Power, 2016).

Potential Problems

The look at potential advantages of group activities painted a very rosy picture. As with other activities that teachers plan, however, group activities do not always succeed as teachers hope they will. This section looks at potential problems with group activities in English language classes.

REFLECTIVE BREAK

What is a negative experience you have had working with other people outside of school situations?

What were you doing?

Why was the experience negative?

Example: *While cleaning your house with your family, one family member mysteriously develops a sore back or suddenly remembers a very important appointment and can no longer help out.*

The following problems may arise when teachers facilitate group activities in English language classes:

- Students learn unproductive target language habits from their peers.

- Students use their first language all the time instead of the target language.

- Students refuse to help their peers.

- Students avoid taking part in the group activities.

- One or two students take over the group activity and do not allow the other group members to take part.

- Students only want to learn from their teachers and, therefore, do not want to interact with their peers.

- Students believe that teachers who use group activities are lazy and irresponsible.

- Students lose motivation when they believe that their grades were lowered by uncooperative or less proficient group members.

- Teachers feel that the class is more difficult to control and monitor when students work in groups.

REFLECTIVE BREAK

Have you ever experienced any of these problems in an English language class, either as a student or a teacher?

Select one of the problems mentioned here or another problem that has arisen when you used group activities with your students. What are two actions you took to lessen or avoid that problem?

Cooperative learning (CL) was developed and continues to be developed as a means of maximizing the potential advantages of group activities and minimizing the potential problems that arise when students learn in groups. The use of CL has been investigated in many countries, across a wide range of subject areas, including second language instruction, and with many ages of students (Johnson & Johnson, 2009). This research provides confidence that CL can be a useful pedagogy.

All classes are different, however, and teachers and students need to determine for themselves whether CL can work in their context. The CL principles described in Chapters 4 and 5 of this book will help you in your exploration. Bear in mind that even if CL is not new for you, it may be new for your students. Thus, you may wish to do the following:

- Explain to students why you are asking them to work together. For instance, you might wish to mention some of the potential advantages discussed in this chapter.

- Share your stories of successful collaboration outside of school, and ask students for theirs.

- Start with tasks that are relatively easy, so students can focus on familiarizing themselves with how to work in groups. This will also build students' confidence in their group and their group mates (Fushino, 2010).

- Do team-building activities, not only when group activities begin but also at other times when groups need a boost.

Activity: A Surprising Fact About Me

A Surprising Fact About Me is a simple team-building activity. The steps follow:

1. Students work alone to think of things about themselves that group mates may not know, for example interesting family members, hobbies, sports, favorite games or food, or wishes for the future.

2. Group members take turns, moving from left to right, to tell group mates their surprising facts.

3. Each turn, after one person has spoken, the person to their right asks a question. Other group members can also ask questions or make comments.

4. Teachers might want to model the process by telling a surprising fact about themselves and teaching students about the various types of questions that can be asked.

 REFLECTIVE BREAK

What is a surprising fact about yourself that you might use to model for your students how to play A Surprising Fact About Me?

What is another team-building activity that might work with your students?

In conclusion, group activities form an essential component of contemporary teaching (Farrell & Jacobs, 2020), as can be seen from a look at most textbooks for English language instruction. Indeed, the dominant paradigm in English language education for many years now, the *communicative approach*, highlights the need for students to be actively engaged in using language to share ideas and information. Groups multiply students' opportunities to engage in such language use. As stated in Chapter 1, to do CL is to do such group activities with thought, thereby increasing the chances of achieving the potential advantages described in the first half of this chapter and decreasing the problems with groups that were described in the second half.

CHAPTER 3

Preparing for Cooperative Learning

This chapter begins with an optimistic picture of a classroom where groups are working well and then proceeds to discuss what elements need to be considered to facilitate such successful peer interactions. Please be clear that there are no rules for how to do cooperative learning (CL); there are only ideas for teachers and students to reflect on as they jointly decide how to best promote student learning in an atmosphere in which both students and teachers enjoy the experience and are motivated to be lifelong learners (Benson, 2011).

Smoothly Functioning Groups

In general, CL groups are long lasting; for instance, they may last for one term or half a term. Sometimes, though, students may come together for just one activity or one day. Whether they are short lived or last an entire term, it is important that groups function smoothly. Observant visitors can walk into a classroom and see that groups are working well, even if the visitors do not speak the language(s) being used in that classroom. Following are some of the typical signs that group activities are functioning smoothly:

- Students are sitting close together so that they can hear each other even while using quiet voices, and they can easily see what group mates are working on, such as a draft of a composition or a website being viewed on an electronic device.

- The class is not quiet; instead, there's a buzzing of conversations. Occasionally, the observers hear laughter or a spirited debate, but the classroom seldom resembles a raucous football stadium.

- All group members appear to be participating fairly equally, with no one excluded and no one seeming to set themselves apart from the group.

- In most cases, each group seems to be a cross section of the overall class. For instance, if the class has a range of nationalities, each group has members from most of those nationalities.

- When the teacher or another student is speaking to the class, students stop what they are doing to watch and listen.

- While groups are working, the teacher is usually seen standing or sitting a bit outside the group. Several minutes may go by before the teacher directly intervenes in a group, and the interventions are often brief. The teacher interventions may be in the form of questions.

 REFLECTIVE BREAK

Have you had the pleasure of witnessing such smoothly functioning group activities?

Four Decision Areas

To set the stage for effective CL, teachers and students need to make decisions in at least four areas: attention signal, the seating arrangement, group size, and group membership. As stated earlier, this book does not consist of inflexible rules that must be followed or else the students are not doing CL. Indeed, teachers can only facilitate cooperation; they cannot impose it, regardless of how many books on CL they have read or how faithfully they implement the ideas in those books. Similarly, teachers cannot make students learn; they can only facilitate students' learning.

The following fictional scenario illustrates this all-too-frequent difference between what teachers teach and what students learn.

There were two friends, Marta and Ana Laura. Every Sunday, Ana Laura would come to Marta's home to go for a walk with Spot, Marta's dog. One Sunday, Ana Laura was happily surprised when Marta told her that the day before, she (Marta) had taught Spot to whistle. When she and Spot returned from their walk, however, Ana Laura looked disappointed. "You said you taught Spot to whistle," she said to Marta. "But during our walk, I kept asking Spot to whistle and he never did."

Sorry," replied Marta. "But I said that I taught Spot to whistle. I didn't say he *learned* to whistle."

Please consider the following ideas presented in this chapter while keeping in mind that any guidelines in this book need to be interpreted through the prism of students' and teachers' contexts.

Attention Signals

Teachers have developed many ways to request students' attention. Among these attention signals are bells and other musical instruments, hand signals, phrases, claps, and raised voices. Whatever attention signal is used, the key is that students understand its purpose, so the class can function efficiently.

 REFLECTIVE BREAK

When students are working in groups, how do you and other teachers you know ask the class for their attention?

Attention signals serve not as devices teachers use to control students. Rather, they serve as tools for the class as a learning community to function better. Students may need to be occasionally reminded of the rationale for the attention signal, and teachers should wait (or repeat the signal) before talking until they have everyone's attention. Last but not least, students can use an attention signal when they lead the class.

One attention signal is for teachers to clap five times and students to clap twice in response. Clapping has advantages over some other signals. Teachers may forget their bells or other items, but their hands are always available. Also, students clapping in response multiplies the sound of the teachers' claps, and clapping encourages students to put down their pencils or pens and take their hands away from their keyboards.

 REFLECTIVE BREAK

One or more of your classes may not need an attention signal, but if a class does need an attention signal, which one would you recommend to the class?

The Seating Arrangement

David Johnson and Roger Johnson head the Cooperative Learning Institute in Minnesota, where they have been leaders in CL since at least the 1970s. During a workshop many years ago, in a bit of an exaggeration, they stated that students should sit "eye to eye, knee to knee; so close they can smell each other." Following are advantages of students sitting close together:

- Students can easily hear each other, even when they speak in quiet voices. Some classes use two levels of voice: a class-sized voice, used when one person is addressing the entire class, and a group-sized voice, used when addressing only one's group mates. Sitting close together allows the quieter group-sized voice to succeed during group activities. Using this quieter voice reduces the overall sound level when groups are interacting.

- Students can see what group mates are doing. This allows students to easily share resources. For example, instead of each student in a group of four having an individual copy of a reading passage, the group can have one copy for every two students (see "Resource Positive Interdependence" in Chapter 4).

- Students have more opportunities to participate in the group, because they are all seated in the heart of the group. Thus, the CL principle of *equal opportunity to participate* (see Chapter 4) is encouraged.

- Students are reminded to participate fully in the group's activities, whereas students on the fringes of the group may be tempted to abstain. Thus, the CL principle of *individual accountability* (see Chapter 4) is encouraged.

REFLECTIVE BREAK

Think of one of your classrooms. You might want to do a drawing of that classroom showing where the students sit and where the teacher normally stands when addressing the class.

- What kind of furniture does the room have?

- How is the furniture usually arranged?

One seating arrangement we favor puts students in groups of four (the next section of this chapter explains why four is recommended). Students sit perpendicular to the front of the room, with the two pairs in each foursome facing each other. Because students are facing each other, a preference for working with peers is promoted; yet, all they need to do is turn sideways to see the front of the room.

REFLECTIVE BREAK

Would the seating arrangement described in the last paragraph work in your classrooms?

If not, how else can the seating be arranged to achieve "eye to eye, knee to knee"?

Group Size

All group sizes have advantages and disadvantages. Larger groups have more hands, hearts, and brains to do tasks and to help any group members who are having difficulty. Also, larger groups mean fewer groups for teachers to supervise. In contrast, smaller groups (and two people are indeed a group) encourage each member to be more active in doing work and making decisions, make it less likely that members will be left out of the group or seek to leave themselves out, and are easier for students to manage.

Our usual favorite group size is four, because foursomes easily divide into pairs, and pairs may be the best size for encouraging maximum student interaction. Each student has the most opportunities to speak in a pair, and students are less likely to be left out. After students have interacted with one group mate, they can continue to share and gather information, ideas, and perspectives by interacting with one or both members of the other twosome in their foursome.

REFLECTIVE BREAK

Of course, a class has only a 25% chance of having exactly four members in each group. What can be done if a class has 35 students, or 33, or any number not divisible by four?

Group Membership

One of the thorniest questions in CL arises over group membership. Some general methods for deciding on group membership are

- *Convenience grouping*: Students form groups with whomever is sitting nearest them.

- *Random grouping*: Often achieved by counting off. For example, in a class of 51, to form foursomes, students could count off to 13. All the 1s form a group, the 2s form a group, and so forth, resulting in 13 groups of four.

- *Student-selected groups*: Students choose their own group mates.

- *Teacher-selected groups*: Teachers use various criteria and their knowledge of their students to decide who will be in which group.

Each of the four methods has its place. Often, students favor student-selected groups, arguing that they work best when they work with people whom they already know and with whom they feel comfortable. However, student-selected groups suffer from two major drawbacks. First, some students may be left out, for instance because they do not yet have friends in the class or because classmates believe they will be a liability to a group because of lack of language proficiency or cooperative skills. Second, student-selected groups often will not be heterogeneous because, as the saying goes, "birds of a feather flock together"—that is, individuals often migrate toward others who share similar characteristics to themselves.

Teacher-selected groups may offer the surest way to form heterogeneous groups. One technique for doing this is to list students from highest to lowest, based on their current language proficiency, using whatever data are available, such as quiz scores or grades from a previous course. The first group of four consists of one student from the top of the proficiency list, one from the bottom and two from the middle. This is where other variables, such as ethnicity, nationality, and gender can come in. Consider organizing groups to maximize the distribution of proficiency levels while also accounting for a diversity of other student features and characteristics within groups.

Also, group formation methods can be combined. For instance, students can choose their group mates but need to follow guidelines for heterogeneity when doing so. For example, each group might need to have members from different countries.

Activity: The Same Game

Heterogeneous groups often consist of students who would not otherwise interact with each other—people who feel they have little or nothing in common other than the fact that they are learning English in the same class. Thus, a team-building activity that highlights similarities might be useful. One example of such a team-building activity is The Same Game. The steps follow:

1. Foursomes divide into groups of two. Each person works alone to write 10 items or activities they like, such as mangoes, mobile phones, playing badminton, and listening to music.

2. Students discuss their lists with their partner and try to find four items or activities that they both like. These four may come from their lists or may emerge from discussion.

3. The foursome comes together and decides on one item or activity that all four group members like. This commonality can be used to form a group name, mascot, or logo.

 REFLECTIVE BREAK

What has been your policy on group formation?

If you wanted your students to be in heterogeneous groups, on what factors would you mix the groups (e.g., proficiency, nationality, gender)?

Technique: Expert Groups Jigsaw

One of the best-known CL techniques, Jigsaw, was specifically created to use heterogeneous groups as a means to advance ties among people of different races (Aronson, 2023). Following are the steps in Jigsaw:

1. Students' regular group is known as their home group. Each home group member receives (or searches for) different material on a related topic. For instance, the common topic might be types of music, and the four different pieces might explain reggae, hip hop, rock, and traditional Chinese music.

2. Students leave their home groups and form expert groups of no more than four members with people with the same piece, for example, a reggae expert group. The goal of the expert groups is twofold: Learn their piece and prepare to teach about it to their home group members.

3. Students thank their expert group members and return to their home groups. There, they take turns to teach their home group members. Each turn includes time for questions, comments, and additions by the other group members, and perhaps by the presenter as well.

4. Students do something that requires information presented by all of the home group members. Typically, this involves an individual quiz. Other possibilities include mindmaps and entries in a reflection journal.

Jigsaw is more complicated than most of the other CL techniques in this book. Here are some pointers:

- One variation on regular Jigsaw is Jigsaw II. In regular Jigsaw, each home group member only has their own piece and is totally dependent on the other home group members for the information in the other pieces. In Jigsaw II, students receive all the pieces and become experts in only one of them.

- Perhaps, the main reason that Jigsaw lessons fail is that students cannot understand their piece and, thus, cannot teach it to their home group members. Ways to avoid the problem include simplifying pieces and providing a glossary. If students are searching for their own materials for Jigsaw instead of using teacher-provided materials, teachers can recommend comprehensible sources, such as websites. Teachers can also introduce students to electronic help tools, such as online dictionaries.

- Another reason Jigsaw fails arises from students' lack of skill in teaching their group mates. For example, some students will just read their piece aloud to their home group members or, even worse, pass their piece to their group mates and ask them to read it. To overcome this, students can use graphic organizers, such as mindmaps, to structure their home group presentations. Also, students should rehearse their presentation in their expert teams before returning home.

 REFLECTIVE BREAK

What is one topic on which your students could do Jigsaw?

What materials would they use?

What might you do to make these materials more comprehensible?

Two Final Points

Two other classroom management issues deserve attention in this chapter on preparations for group activities. First, some groups and individuals often finish before others. To prepare for this occurrence, classes need *sponge activities*, activities that "soak up" this extra time. Sponge activities may be generic or specific. Generic sponges fit almost any context and may include helping another group or person who is still working or continuing with one's extensive reading book. Specific sponges link directly to the activity students have just finished.

A second classroom management issue is time limits. Giving time limits makes it more likely that groups will finish at the same time and also helps groups plan their time and stay on task. Of course, time limits should be flexibly applied.

CHAPTER 4

Four Teaching Principles for Interaction

What can make cooperative learning (CL) more than just an arrangement of furniture in which small groups of students sit together? This chapter examines four CL principles that endeavor to transform a group into more than the sum of its parts. These four principles are

1. maximum peer interactions

2. equal opportunity to participate

3. individual accountability, and

4. positive interdependence.

Maximum Peer Interactions (Quantity)

The CL principle of *maximum peer interactions* has two parts: quantity and quality. What could be changed in the following scenario?

> A class of 40 forms five groups of eight members each. After a quick group discussion, the teacher calls on a student from each group to present the group's answer. Another time, each group comes to the front of the class to present.

One potential weakness in this scenario lies in the fact that not much talking time is provided to each of the students in the class. During the group activity, only 12.5% (1 out of 8) of the students are speaking. Then, when the teacher calls on one student per group to report to the class, only one student in the entire class is talking. The same lack of student talk exists when one group at a time speaks to the entire class from the front of the room—2.5% (1 out of 40)—although some students may be carrying on side conversations with those next to them because they may have become bored listening to so many presentations on the same topic.

Although large groups and whole-class presentations do have benefits, alternatives should be considered. With pairs, 50% (1 out of 2) of the students are speaking. Thus, in the class of 40, 20 peer interactions are taking place. This is substantially more than the 12.5% (five peer interactions) with groups of eight. Then, during the reporting phase of the activity, if twosomes report to the other pair in their foursome, 25% (1 out of 4) of the students are speaking; in other words, 10 peer interactions. This is substantially more than the 2.5%, only one peer interaction, when one student reports to the entire class.

The preceding example illustrates the importance of the principle of *maximum peer interactions (quantity)*. This principle guides teachers and students in how to realize one advantage of groups mentioned in Chapter 2: that students use the target language more. Teachers can easily see if maximum peer interactions (quantity) has been successfully implemented. All they need to do is look around the class and ask themselves, "How many peer interactions are taking place?"

Technique: Write-Pair-Switch

Write-Pair-Switch does a particularly good job of bringing to life the principle of maximum peer interactions (quantity). The steps follow:

1. Work alone to write an answer.

2. Pair with a partner to share and discuss answers.

3. Then, find another partner from within your group. Tell your new partner about your old partner's answer and the discussion you had about it.

 REFLECTIVE BREAK

How does Write-Pair-Switch bring to life the principle of maximum peer interactions (quantity)? (To help you answer this question, calculate how many peer interactions are taking place in a class of 40 in the second and third steps of Write-Pair-Switch.)

Maximum Peer Interactions (Quality)

The twin of maximum peer interaction (quantity) is *maximum peer interaction (quality)*. The following story illustrates what a group might look like when maximum peer interaction (quality) has been neglected.

> A group of students is doing Write-Pair-Switch. Their task is to answer a set of questions that the class generated after reading and discussing a short text. At the pair step, students pass each other their written answers, but little discussion takes place and students only write "very good" next to their partners' answers. In the switch step, students read aloud their first partner's answer to their new partner.

Much of the magic of CL takes place when students discuss with each other. As noted in Chapter 2, a potential advantage of group activities lies in students' receiving individual attention from peers, much more individual attention than one teacher could possibly provide. In the scenario described here, though, peer interactions take place but have little quality. Quality interactions include features such as group members' seeking and providing help, pushing each other to think more deeply (such as by asking for reasons and examples), disagreeing with each other in a collegial manner, and evaluating each other's work to improve it. Thus, with CL, teachers do more than look around the room and ask, "How many peer interactions are taking place?" Teachers must also ask, "Are these quality peer interactions?"

Equal Opportunity to Participate

All too often, group activities look like this:

> Students in groups of four are working on a mindmap about food. However, in one group, three students have seized all the marker pens and are doing all the drawing. The other group member is ignored whenever she wants to draw or even contribute an idea for what to draw. Why is she being excluded? Her English is not as good as that of her group mates. Also, the other three are already friends, but the fourth is not part (at least not yet) of their friendship group.

When one or more members are excluded from a group, those excluded lose learning opportunities, and the group loses their input. This is why the principle of *equal opportunity to participate* constitutes a basic part of CL. For various reasons, even under ideal conditions, participation seldom will be exactly equal, but the possibility for relatively equal output from each group member should be there.

Technique: Circle of Speakers

One simple way that CL attempts to roughly equalize participation is via turn-taking CL techniques such as Circle of Speakers (Jacobs et al., 2022), which can be done in groups of two, three, or four and looks like this:

1. Teachers or students develop questions or tasks. Students may have a bit of time to think and possibly write before the peer interaction begins.

2. Students take turns in the order they are seated to contribute to the discussion. This taking of turns can go on for multiple rounds. Student turns can be responses to previous contributions.

3. The teacher calls a number, and the person with that number shares a partner's idea or some other part of the group discussion with the rest of the class. They do not just report what they themselves said.

Variation: To further equalize participation in Circle of Speakers and other CL techniques, each turn can be timed (e.g., 15 seconds).

 REFLECTIVE BREAK

What is a specific example of how you might use Circle of Speakers the next time you teach?

With many CL techniques, teachers can use a simple formula to create activities:

Step 1—Take any activity (e.g., from a textbook or online).

Step 2—Add a CL technique, such as Write-Pair-Switch.

Step 3—You now have a CL activity.

The point is that you do not need to create a CL activity from scratch; you can repurpose activities your students have used previously via other instructional modes, such as teacher-fronted or individual. Perhaps your students often engage in group discussions, but without the benefit of CL principles. All of these can easily become CL activities.

Individual Accountability

What is wrong with this scenario?

> A group is scheduled to make a presentation in class this afternoon. Yesterday, they discussed what each group member would do, and yesterday evening they were supposed to e-mail each other to share feedback on their parts. Unfortunately, Haryanto never e-mailed the other group members or replied to their e-mails, and this morning, when the others asked him what had happened, he told them he was busy playing a video game with some friends. He invited the others to play the game with him online tonight.

The CL principle of equal opportunity to participate attempts to give everyone a chance to take an active role in their group. Conversely, the CL principle of *individual accountability* seeks to encourage all members to make the most of that opportunity to participate and, thereby, share their ideas and energy with the group. In the story, Haryanto decided to use his ideas and energy elsewhere.

Among the ways that CL encourages each student to feel individual accountability to their group are the following:

- Each group member takes a turn, such as in Circle of Speakers.

- Each group member has a role to play, such as questioner (whose job is to ask questions), praiser (who highlights what group mates have done well), encourager (who encourages quieter members to take part in the group activities), and facilitator (who keeps the group on track toward completing their tasks).

- After the group activity, everyone takes an individual quiz or does some other individual task, or the teacher calls on group members at random to present and explain their group's ideas.

Technique: Everyone Can Explain

A CL technique that encourages individual accountability is Everyone Can Explain. The steps follow:

1. Groups work together on a task. Each student has a number, such as 1, 2, 3, or 4.

2. They develop a response(s) for that task.

3. They check that everyone in the group can give and explain the group's ideas. (This is why the CL technique is called "Everyone Can Explain.")

4. The teacher calls a number at random to explain what their group has done.

5. If classmates and the teacher like the answer, they praise the group mates for preparing the presenter well.

 REFLECTIVE BREAK

What are various ways that the CL techniques in this book and elsewhere promote equal opportunity to participate and individual accountability?

Positive Interdependence

What is wrong with this scenario?

> Students are seated in groups of four, doing an assignment in their textbook. The assignment is not an easy one, at least not for a couple of the students, and it is to be handed in at the end of class. Despite the difficulty of the task and the fact that the group members are seated together, they are not working together. The only discussion occurs when one student borrows stationery supplies from a group mate.

The tie that binds group members together, the glue that encourages students to stick with their group members even when difficulties arise, is called *positive interdependence*. Positive interdependence amounts to a feeling among group mates that everyone is important and necessary and that what helps one member helps others and what hurts one group member hurts the rest. To borrow from literature to explain positive interdependence, the title characters of Alexandre Dumas' novel, *The Three Musketeers*, would say, "All for one, one for all." A more modern saying is, "Everyone wins or no one wins." From another perspective, statisticians would describe the feeling of positive interdependence by stating that students feel that their outcomes are positively correlated with those of their group mates.

In the scenario at the beginning of this section, students did not seem to feel positively interdependent. The task was challenging for at least two of the group members, yet assistance was neither sought nor offered. What is the point of being in groups if students are not going to cooperate? In this case, grouping has become no more than a furniture arrangement.

Fortunately, CL literature offers many ideas for promoting the feeling of positive interdependence among group members. Here are seven of these ideas:

Goal Positive Interdependence

The group has a common goal or goals, and the members know that they have to work together to achieve the goal(s). For example, they need to create a crossword puzzle for other groups to play.

Reward Positive Interdependence

The group members celebrate or receive a reward when they reach their group goal(s). Either they all celebrate, or no one celebrates. For example, the group's goal might be to read a certain number of books as part of their extensive reading program. When they reach their goal, all the group members enjoy an additional 10 minutes of silent reading time.

Resource Positive Interdependence

Group members have different resources, and they need to share these resources for the group to reach its goal. Resources can be information or materials. The CL technique Jigsaw (see Chapter 3) highlights the use of information resources to encourage group members to feel positive interdependence. Similarly, imagine a group of four working to plan a birthday party. One member has information about how to make a present from reused materials, another will be in charge of cooperative games at the party, another will find out about dances that someone in a wheelchair can do, and the fourth member is in charge of finding a venue and inviting others to the party. To plan the party, they need to share the information they each have.

Role Positive Interdependence

Each group member has a role that is important to the success of the group. For instance, in the birthday party example, students could have the rotating roles of leader, controversy captain (who disagrees politely with others' ideas as to where to have the party, how to make the present, what games games to play, and which dances to do), thanker (who thanks others for contributing to the group), and observer (who checks to see if group members successfully use a language point, such as past tense, on which their group has chosen to focus).

Fantasy Positive Interdependence

Setting up an imagined situation is one more way to promote positive interdependence. Group members can fantasize that they are different beings, in a different time, or in a different place. For instance, students can imagine that they are nonhuman animals whom humans frequently eat, such as chickens. The group's task is to convince humans to stop eating chickens.

Identity Positive Interdependence

Members share a common identity, just as a sports team has its team name and mascot and a company or other organization has a logo and slogan. Sharing a common identity helps build solidarity among group members.

Outside Challenge Positive Interdependence

Groups can compete against other groups to see which group scores the most points during a class quiz, for instance. Or, groups can cooperate as a class to overcome a common challenge. For example, the entire class can compete against world hunger by trying to see how much money they can raise as a class to donate to the United Nations' Food and Agriculture Organization.

 REFLECTIVE BREAK

What are various ways that the CL techniques in this book and elsewhere promote a feeling of positive interdependence among students?

Knowledge of the various types of positive interdependence enables teachers and students to convert instructional techniques designed to be done alone into CL activities. For instance, K-W-L (Ogle, 1986) is a well-known reading technique. The letters *K*, *W*, and *L* stand for what I *know*, what I *want* to know, and what I *learned* with the following steps:

1. The class decides to read about a particular topic.

2. Students work alone to list what they currently know on the topic and how they learned it.

3. Students individually list what they want to know about the topic.

4. The class all read the same text on the topic.

5. Students work alone to write what they learned.

Whole-class discussion may occur in Steps 1, 3, and 5, and even without teacher encouragement, students might consult with peers. However, one way to make K-W-L into more of a CL activity is for students to complete Steps 2, 3, and 4 with peers. For instance, students could initially work alone to list what they know on the topic, and then, they could share that with their partner(s). This could be called Write-Circle of Speakers, because students first write, before taking turns to discuss with their partner(s).

 REFLECTIVE BREAK

In what other ways could K-W-L be modified to apply the principles of CL?

What is another activity in your teaching materials that could be adapted into a CL activity?

CHAPTER 5

Four Teaching Principles for Bonding

What can facilitate collegial relations not just among members of small classroom groups but also between members of different classroom groups? This chapter examines four cooperative learning (CL) principles that build skills and attitudes which enable students to work cooperatively with anyone. These four principles are

1. group autonomy,

2. heterogeneous grouping,

3. cooperation as a value, and

4. using cooperative skills.

Group Autonomy

What is wrong with this scenario?

Students in a class of 34 work in groups of two on a task. The teacher circulates around the room, ready to assist whenever students raise their hand, or whenever the teacher sees or hears an error or wants to praise something students have done. Students look immediately to the teacher when they have a question or want feedback on their work. Soon, so many students have their hands up that the poor teacher feels as though he should take off his shoes and put on a pair of roller blades to glide quickly enough around the class to visit all the students. As the class continues, despite the teacher's best efforts, not only does the sea of hands not wane, but it is now accompanied by a disjointed chorus of students calling plaintively for the teacher to make an urgent desk call to provide them with individual attention.

Situations such as this have led to the adoption of classroom policies such as Team Then Teacher (TTT), meaning that students should seek help and feedback from group mates before turning to the teacher. Taking TTT a step further is the 3 + 1 B4 T policy, which suggests that students first turn to their three (or however many) group mates. If that does not suffice, student should try the 1, meaning one other group before (B4) seeking assistance from teachers (T). The CL principle here is *group autonomy*; in other words, group members as individuals as well as groups should look to peers as their first resort when they want to discuss their work. Yes, teachers are most certainly still there, but not as the first option.

A key way to promote the CL principle of group autonomy and perhaps the most important point to remember when planning CL activities relates to whether the tasks that groups take on can be done. Yes, as the sayings go, "Two heads are better than one" and "Many hands make light work," but even multiple heads and hands are unlikely to be able to do magic and to, for example, convert a task appropriate to an intermediate-level class into a task that a beginning-level class can handle. Thus, tasks or materials may need to be modified, or some other form of assistance should be provided. Such assistance might include the following:

- Students use reference materials, such as electronic dictionaries.

- Students receive answer keys and, for example, one member of each pair does the even number questions while the other does the odd number questions, and each has suggested answers for their partner's questions.

- Students see annotated models or rubrics.

- Groups that finish early help those groups still working.

- The task is the latter part of a series of tasks that build in difficulty.

- The groups are heterogeneous as to past achievement in English, so that those currently more proficient in English can aid those whose current proficiency level is lower.

- Students have learned cooperative skills that enable their groups to function more effectively.

Technique: Exchange a Question

Group autonomy fits well with CL, because CL seeks to empower students—to help them become lifelong learners who can continue to grow their knowledge and skills without the constant presence of classroom teachers (Little, 2022). One CL technique that seeks to make students less dependent on teachers is Exchange a Question. In this technique, instead of teachers and teaching materials being the sole source of questions, students generate questions for themselves and their peers. Following are the steps in Exchange a Question:

1. The class discusses types of questions. For example, in reading, the answers to some questions can be found directly in the text. Such questions are sometimes called *text retrieval questions*. In contrast, for other questions, students need to go beyond the information given to them in the text. These latter questions are sometimes called *thinking questions*.

2. Students work alone to generate one or more questions related to what the class has been studying.

3. On a separate paper or on their electronic device, students write possible answers to their questions.

4. Students exchange questions but not answers.

5. Students answer each other's questions and then compare answers.

The CL principle of group autonomy also comes into play when teachers circulate among the groups during a CL activity. Teachers and students easily fall back into old habits and make teachers the center of attention. To move students into the spotlight, teachers need to resist the temptation to rush in to immediately save students at the first sign of error or doubt. Instead, groups should be given space to figure out how to move forward, space to discover and amend their own mistakes.

REFLECTIVE BREAK

What is your approach to helping students who are having difficulties?

Heterogeneous Grouping

What is wrong with this scenario?

> One of many reasons Ms. Adelina enjoys teaching her class is the rich mix of students, with a variety of Middle Eastern and Latin American countries represented. To her dismay, however, outside the classroom students from one geographic region do not mix with their classmates from the other. She sees many students studying together in the library, but these out-of-class study groups are homogeneous as to geographic region. Even in the classroom, unless Ms. Adelina intervenes, although her students are generally friendly and outgoing, the students will normally only talk to others from their region.

REFLECTIVE BREAK

Have you experienced student self-segregation by a particular characteristic (e.g., gender, race, home language)? What was the characteristic, and if you addressed the self-segregation, how did you address it?

The CL principle of *heterogeneous grouping* received extensive treatment in Chapter 3 in the section "Group Membership." To summarize, usually groups should represent a cross section of the class. For example, if half of the students are from the Middle East and the other half are from Latin America, each group might include two people from the Middle East and two from Latin America in addition to each group having a range of proficiency levels.

Two goals motivate the formation of heterogeneous groups. First, by mixing proficiency levels, teachers hope to encourage peer tutoring. As noted earlier in this chapter, one teacher can provide only limited assistance to a class full of students, but their group mates are right there to help. Plus, this peer help is not one-way assistance; when students teach via elaborations, such as explanations and examples, both of the group members benefit: those being helped and the ones receiving help. The latter student benefits because "those who teach learn twice."

REFLECTIVE BREAK

What is an example of how you personally have experienced "Those who teach learn twice," that is, when you learned by teaching others?

Example: *In teaching writing, teachers may learn or at least be reminded of guidelines for good writing, such as making clear connections between sentences and between paragraphs.*

Social harmony represents a second goal that motivates the CL principle of heterogeneous grouping. Indeed, one of the scholars whom many point to as an inspiration for CL was the social psychologist Kurt Lewin (see Marrow, 1977, for a biography). Lewin and those who followed in his tradition sought to understand how to overcome prejudice and bring together diverse groups of people. For instance, Eliot Aronson, the founder of Jigsaw (see Chapter 3), developed the technique in response to the fact that students of different ethnic groups did not mix outside of class. He and his colleagues reasoned that if teachers could bring diverse students together in the classroom in a spirit of positive interdependence, the feeling of camaraderie might sustain outside the classroom.

Cooperation as a Value

This scenario has much to like.

Mr. Marino and his colleagues started CL in September. Now, in February, after some ups and downs and twists and turns, the groups are working together well. Mr. Marino feels especially gratified when he observes quality peer interactions among his students, as they spur each other to think more deeply and use the target language to express their thinking. Mr. Marino and his colleagues have now decided to work on spreading the feeling of positive interdependence to the whole class, the whole school, and beyond. For instance, rather than only having learning goals for individual groups (see "Goal Positive Interdependence" in Chapter 4), class and school goals are also created, such as a target number of extensive reading books the entire class and entire school will read. To extend students' circle of concern beyond the school, Mr. Marino's class has decided to examine the case of wild-caught dolphins who are being exploited to entertain people in his school's city. The class will study and discuss the issue, and each student will be encouraged to take action based on their own view. Other classes have decided on other issues.

As is evident in the story from Mr. Marino's school, CL encompasses important social and affective goals, as well as cognitive goals, such as raising test scores. This attention to social and affective objectives along with cognitive ones fits with the CL principle of *cooperation as a value*, inspired by John Dewey. In addition to Lewin, Dewey stands out as another early 20th-century scholar whose influence can be seen in CL. The following quote from a collection of Dewey's writings clearly signals his preference for cooperation:

> [T]he schools, through reliance upon the spur of competition and the bestowing of special honors and prizes, only build up and strengthen the disposition that makes an individual when he leaves school employ his special talents and superior skill to outwit his fellow without respect for the welfare of others. (as cited in Archambault, 1964, p. 11)

Education, to Dewey, should serve the greater good and make society a better place. Thus, students learn not primarily for themselves. In Dewey's own words,

> There is no greater egoism than that of learning when it is treated simply as a mark of personal distinction to be held and cherished for its own sake. [K]nowledge is a possession held in trust for the furthering of the well-being of all. (as cited in Archambault, 1964, p. 12)

Technique: Circle of Writers

Bringing social issues into education, as Dewey suggested, can be especially easy for language teachers because, as Rivers (1976) noted, "As language teachers we are the most fortunate of teachers—all subjects are ours" (p. 96). One CL technique that can be used here is Circle of Writers (Jacobs et al., 2022). The following is one version of that technique, known as Circle of Writers (One at a Time):

1. Each group of two, three, or four students has only one piece of paper.

2. Each student is assigned a number within the group.

3. Each student takes a turn to write before passing the paper to another member of the group. This writing can continue what the previous person wrote or can provide feedback on a previous idea.

4. The paper can circulate around the group multiple times.

5. Later, a number is called. The student with that number reports on one or more of their group's ideas.

Another version of this activity is Circle of Writers (All at Once). In this case, instead of one paper per group, there is one paper per group member. Generally, students use the All at Once version when they are going to write more than a few words or a quick idea. For example, each student can start a story. After an amount of time, e.g., 3 minutes, everyone passes the paper to the person on their right. When students receive their groupmate's paper, they read what is written, check if anything is not clear, and then continue, but do not end, the story. This "pass, read, check, write, and pass again" procedure continues until the papers are back with the people who started the stories. Those people finish the stories and then share, by reading aloud or passing the papers, with the rest of the group.

Using Cooperative Skills

Because this is the eighth and final CL principle to be discussed in this book, we will end with a positive word picture, a picture that captures the promise of CL.

Ms. Fong cannot help smiling when she sees her class do CL now. What a difference from when the year started! They are now so polite to their classmates and their teachers (at least on good days), with many thanks expressed, praises given, invitations to speak extended, and requests for clarification made. But there is an even more impressive part of what these students have accomplished with the guidance of several of their teachers who have worked in unison with their school's principal. When listening to these students interact, Ms. Fong also hears students promoting deeper thinking by checking that their group mates understand, disagreeing sometimes strenuously but usually politely, and asking each other to explain or to think aloud as they do a task. One can still hear language errors when students use these cooperative skills, but the spirit of cooperation shines through and the language continues to improve.

As the story about Ms. Fong's class demonstrates, groups function better when students know and use cooperative skills. A very short list of such skills, in addition to the ones in the preceding story, includes listening attentively, requesting examples, asking others to speak louder, pointing out possible places for improvement, and keeping a group on task. Often, explicit instruction about why and how to use these skills aids students in making cooperative skills a natural part of their language learning repertoire.

Fortunately for language classes, cooperative skills can often be incorporated in the regular syllabus. A six-step procedure for teaching cooperative skills is as follows:

1. Students understand the need for a particular skill.

2. The class discusses the words, tone of voice, and body language associated with the skill.

3. The class practices the skill in isolation from course content, such as by role-playing or playing a game that uses the skill.

4. Groups practice the skill during their regular class activities and monitor their use of the skill.

5. Groups discuss how well they have used the skill and how they might improve their use of the skill.

6. The class continues working on the same cooperative skill until students are content with their level of use of the skill.

REFLECTIVE BREAK

What is one cooperative skill that would enable your students to work together more effectively?

Would the six-step procedure described here help them to make that cooperative skill a regular part of how they interact with others?

Technique: Think-Aloud Pairs

Thinking aloud offers students a means of practicing the cooperative skills of sharing one's thinking with others and of giving feedback to others. In thinking aloud, students give voice to what is going on in their minds as they complete a task. This verbalized thinking can include emotions as well as cognitive thoughts. Think-Aloud Pairs is one CL technique specifically designed to include thinking aloud. Here is how it works:

1. Each group of four begins as two pairs, each doing the same tasks.

2. In each pair, the roles of thinker and coach regularly rotate. Thinkers express what is happening in their minds as they do the tasks, and coaches provide encouragement and feedback.

3. After a certain amount of time or number of tasks, the two pairs in the foursome discuss their responses and try to reach consensus.

4. After the discussion, they thank each other for their ideas and go back to thinking aloud with their one partner.

CHAPTER 6

Cooperative Learning and Positive Psychology

This chapter attempts to explore cooperative learning (CL) through the lens of positive psychology, which is the scientific study of how we live a meaningful life (Seligman, 2011; Seligman & Adler, 2019). A relatively new branch of psychology, positive psychology began as an antidote to mainstream or traditional psychology, which tends to focus on the negative—on people's problems and disorders and attempts to find solutions. In contrast, positive psychology focuses on people's positive traits and on what makes them happy and satisfied. The goal is to build on the positive, to make it even better, and to use it to overcome problems, helping oneself and others.

Reading through this chapter, you may be surprised to find close connections between CL and positive psychology. In fact, they share philosophical roots and integrate a set of common perspectives, values, and objectives into their approaches. We believe that CL with positive psychological underpinnings can provide a foundation for enhancing the future of language teaching and learning.

First, CL helps students enjoy learning. In this sense, it mirrors the objectives of positive psychology. We learn better when we enjoy something and continue learning and practicing what we enjoy. Teachers need to strategically design learning environments to leverage both the cognitive and affective aspects of learning. The principles we discussed in Chapters 4 and 5 guide students to feel intrinsically motivated to learn with others.

CL and positive psychology both have roots in a humanistic approach to education. Humanists believe the objectives of education should be to improve their own lives and personal growth, and to improve the lives of others in their communities. As such, proponents of both CL and positive psychology consider the promotion of learners' well-being to be a legitimate goal of education; thus, they take a dual-strand approach, pursuing both academic and nonacademic goals. One of the CL principles for bonding (Chapter 5) is using cooperative skills, such as listening attentively to group mates, using people's names when talking to them, waiting patiently, and disagreeing politely. Not only are these skills crucial for small groups to effectively function and learn academic content, but they are also indispensable to a good life, which is beyond specific academic goals.

Cooperative skills can be developed. Likewise, character strengths can be cultivated throughout a lifetime. As such, both CL and positive psychology use a growth mindset—an underlying belief that we possess the potential to further improve the quality of our characters and our skills (Dweck, 2017). In families, schools, and communities, useful skills and positive character strengths are teachable and learnable. This belief is supported by recent findings in neuroscience that our brains are malleable and that, with practice, we can increase and strengthen the neural connections between what we do, think, and feel. Both CL and positive psychology hold a future-oriented view of human learning. Tomorrow, we will be able to do alone what we did with others today.

In fact, this very idea brings us to the next theme. Although CL has a strong social orientation (Tomasello, 2009; Wolf & Tomasello, 2020) as we have seen in Chapter 2, it also aims to make individuals stronger (Johnson & Johnson, 2009). In productive groups, members work together to accomplish shared goals. These cooperative achievements are positively interdependent. Each member achieves their own goals if, and only if, the other group members do so as well (Chapter 4). In this sense, cooperative groups constitute a dynamic whole. Positive psychology pursues individual well-being, but individual well-being depends to a large extent on positive social relationships. In fact, Seligman's (2011) PERMA model includes relationships in five key characteristics of well-being (the four other characteristics are positive emotion, engagement, meaning, and accomplishments). Satisfying and meaningful lives take root only in communities. When people contribute to the well-being of others, they themselves live a good life. Both CL and positive psychology stem from the observation that our need to connect with others is fundamental and powerful.

Although CL offers many techniques for creating well-functioning groups, it also acknowledges obstacles. We have already pointed out advantages and potential problems of student interaction in Chapter 2. For example, though CL values different perspectives among group members, differences might create tension. A case in point can be seen when some group members are less interested in learning and may sometimes be disrespectful toward other members. However, these problems offer opportunities for growth. Members learn from overcoming interpersonal problems they encounter, and they develop cooperative skills in this process (Johnson et al., 2021). Adversity facilitates growth as individuals and as group members. Similarly, although positive psychology explores what is going right, it does not dismiss what is going wrong. Positive psychology does not disregard negative emotions or experiences; in fact, it values adversity to promote well-being. Thus, both CL and positive psychology see value in positive and negative experiences and share both idealistic and realistic perspectives on how we live and grow.

Lastly, both CL and positive psychology appreciate diversity and variability. Cooperative principles look like a recipe for success, but in fact they do not provide a quick panacea. Every group is unique with members having different personalities, experiences, and strengths; thus, CL principles and techniques work for each group in different ways. There are no identical groups. Similarly, positive psychology claims that many different pathways exist to living a meaningful life. For example, there are not fixed sets of character strengths to enhance well-being, and people can be happy with different configurations of characteristics. Put simply, people and groups can flourish in a variety of ways.

Now, we look at the two positive psychology interventions (Seligman, 2011) that can be applied to second language learning in a cooperative way.

Activity: Circle of Interviewers—Expressing Gratitude

Being thankful for others makes us appreciate what we have experienced in life.

1. Students write thank-you notes to a specific person or a group of people.

2. For less proficient learners, teachers can give a sentence template, such as "I'm thankful for _____ because _____" (Helgesen, 2019, p. 79).

3. In groups of four, students form two pairs.

4. One student interviews their partner about someone they would like to thank and why. The partners then exchange roles.

5. In their foursomes, an individual from each pair reports what they have learned from their gratitude interview of their initial partner.

6. Members ask follow-up questions.

Activity: Forward Snowball—Three Good Things

Recognizing good things in life also contributes to our well-being.

1. As homework, students write three good things that happened to them in the past 24 hours.

2. Pairs explain their own lists to each other and make a combined list, with no duplications, of good things.

3. Two pairs get together and make a longer combined list. Students can meet with other pairs to grow their lists larger and larger, just like a snowball grows larger and larger as it rolls down a hill.

 REFLECTIVE BREAK

A *haiku* is a three-line, structured poem: the first line has five syllables, the second seven, and the third five. Please write a *haiku* to express feelings you had while reading this chapter (Helgesen, 2019, pp. 27–29).

Examples:

When people help you	Going to the sea
Say with a big sunny smile	I want to swim like a fish
"Thank you very much."	But I cannot swim

Check out the website ELT and Happiness (www.eltandhappiness.com) and find an activity you like. You may want to adjust it to suit your students. Explain how you do it and why.

CHAPTER 7

Student–Student Interaction in Virtual Classrooms

Throughout this book, we have focused on face-to-face interactions and the advantages of learning together in small groups. However, at the onset of the COVID-19 pandemic in 2020, teachers all over the world had no choice but to adapt to online platforms and make use of new communication technologies. Furthermore, even without a pandemic, online learning offers many advantages. This chapter explores how we can facilitate cooperative learning (CL) in virtual environments.

Students might be comfortable with CL group activities in traditional in-person classrooms, but not in online environments. Teachers should (1) strategically structure group activities to facilitate students' participation and interaction without teachers' direct involvement, and (2) provide opportunities and ample time for students to foster social networks and refine cooperative skills. With these guidelines in place, virtual platforms can serve the development of learner autonomy.

Planning and Virtual Classroom Management

Planning plays a more significant role in teaching online than in-person. In virtual learning environments, it becomes even more important that all students understand what they might be able to do by the end of an activity and how they might be able to do it (Johnson et al., 2021). Although the same issue can arise with face-to-face teaching, in virtual groupwork, small ambiguities can even more easily lead to confusion. As a result, instructions for online group activities should be simple and clear so that every student is more likely to understand the activity's process and purpose. For instance, CL activities are designed with the hope that no one is left out or free-rides, and that everyone has a stake in helping others.

Teachers should make wise choices for specific activities from the wide array of CL techniques, such as Circle of Speakers, Circle of Writers, and Everyone Can Explain, to name just a few. These techniques promote the equal participation and contribution of all students to their group. It is a good idea to examine each of your planned online activities with regard to the four CL principles for interaction discussed in Chapter 4 (maximum peer interactions, equal opportunities to participate, individual accountability, and positive interdependence). These principles facilitate interaction to make students' contributions more equitable, more beneficial, and more in-depth. In addition, each member playing a distinct role in their group can aid the attainment of those four CL principles.

In face-to-face classrooms, if teachers notice that some groups are having trouble, they can easily jump in and help a particular group or make suggestions to the whole class. However, in virtual classrooms, it is more difficult for teachers to monitor how well groups are functioning. On platforms like Zoom, teachers can visit one group at a time, but they cannot keep an eye on all groups at once. To address this gap, teachers might want to review the goal(s) and procedures of each activity with the whole class before groups start working. Careful and elaborate planning and clear instructions are often keys to success—and this is particularly true in virtual classrooms. At the same time, teachers might be pleasantly surprised by the variations that students intentionally or unintentionally develop.

Meaningful learning takes place in safe environments where students connect emotionally with each other (Tokuhama-Espinosa, 2021). In a study done by the authors of this book, along with a colleague (Jacobs et al., 2016), we found evidence of incivility in face-to-face interactions among students at a Japanese women's university, a place where, according to stereotypes, politeness should prevail. On the internet, reports of cyber bullying and other forms of incivility have become common. Therefore, the CL principle of *cooperative skills* may be especially important to the creation of safe learning environments for virtual learning.

Additionally, students' need to socialize cannot be overlooked nor downplayed in virtual classrooms, where students are geographically scattered. As discussed in Chapter 2, proximity is one of the key elements to facilitate cooperation among group mates. Thus, in virtual environments, students benefit from ample time to get to know each other using ice-breaking and team-building activities. Such a practice promotes group autonomy, one of the four cooperative principles for bonding discussed in Chapter 5. Simple ice-breaking activities, such as sharing what they regularly do in their free time using the Circle of Interviewers, can create "joint intentions and commitments" (Tomasello, 2009, p. xiii), which promote sharing of ideas and mutual helping. Personalizing these activities also leads to greater socialization and emotional engagement among students, encouraging feelings of safety and comfort among group members.

Online environments have some obvious restrictions, such as making it more difficult to indicate objects for joint attention, share resources, and notice nonverbal cues (e.g., body movements and gestures), which may be out of sight. However, these restrictions can produce good learning opportunities to refine pragmatic language knowledge. For example, students can learn different degrees of politeness and distinct tones of voice during negotiations. Waiting patiently for others to speak and encouraging quiet members to speak might be more difficult in virtual settings, but it is still possible. In online classrooms, students can learn to be less dependent on the para-linguistic components of communication. We need to keep in mind that people are social by nature and will, therefore, need to nurture skills to work positively and productively with others in virtual communities and recognize cooperation as a value. In fact, cooperative skills in virtual communication are an undoubtedly necessary part of 21st-century skills.

Despite these difficulties, virtual learning environments bring some advantages for meaningful cooperation in small groups. Heterogeneous grouping, another CL principle for bonding, is easier in virtual classrooms when using a random grouping function. Have you experienced feeling somewhat irritated when students are slow in moving around the classroom to form new groups? This does not happen in virtual classrooms, because forming groups takes a matter of seconds. Next, students can usually show their names on the screen, making it easier to address each other by name. Furthermore, using the chat function, teachers can keep everyone involved. For example, teachers can type a question and ask all the students to respond. Then, teachers can integrate these responses into the next group activity. In this way, classroom activities become more dynamic and democratic. In cooperative virtual classrooms, teachers can quickly and easily shift back and forth between a whole-class meeting, group sessions, and individual learning.

Lastly, teaching and learning in virtual environments is expected to yield important benefits (Ivone et al., 2020; Santosa et al., 2022). We have referred to group autonomy as one of the principles for students' bonding. In fact, it is also regarded as a first step toward learner autonomy or agency. Students become less dependent on the teacher in cooperative groups, because they can turn to their group mates before asking their teacher for support. This is one step toward learner autonomy. Self-knowledge, which is indispensable for learner autonomy, also increases through social interaction (Tokuhama-Espinosa, 2021). We come to know ourselves not just by introspection but also by others' evaluation of us, as we see ourselves reflected through the eyes of others (Leary, 1995). CL seems to prioritize group learning, but in fact it prioritizes making individual students stronger in the process. Virtual environments can contribute to this vital goal of education.

 REFLECTIVE BREAK

Design simple ice-breaking questions that take advantage of the constraints of virtual environments.

Example: *What do I have in my hands (off screen)? What do you have on your desk (off screen)?*

Choose a few cooperative games and modify them for virtual classrooms.

Cooperative Games in Virtual Classrooms

Many games work equally as well in virtual environments as in traditional classrooms. To have a cooperative game does not necessarily mean creating an entirely new game. Instead, a competitive game can be easily changed into a cooperative game. The easiest way to do this is to not keep score; students just play for the fun of it: fun for the social interaction and fun for the cognitive stimulation. First, for example, try Spot the Difference. This is played as follows: Taking turns, students switch their cameras off, then change their posture, outfits, or objects visible on screen, before switching their cameras on again. Other group members then attempt to identify the difference their classmate created while off screen.

Pictionary, also known as Win Lose or Draw, is usually played competitively. However, if students do not keep score, they can relax, have fun, and cooperate with each other. For those readers of this book who may not be familiar with Pictionary, the first step is to assemble a flock of vocabulary items, each written on a separate piece of paper, which is then folded. These items can be ones the class is trying to learn. One group member of a team is given a vocabulary item; the rest cannot see the item. The one member does a drawing to represent the item, and the rest of the group tries to guess which vocabulary item is being drawn. Because in this version of Pictionary there are no scores and no losers, students may be more likely to share tips on drawing and guessing.

Finally, Forward Snowball (see Chapter 6) is an excellent game showing that two heads are better than one. A fun variation on this game is to start with a relatively long word, such as *cooperation*. The goal is to spell as many different words as possible from the letters in the target word. Because *cooperation* has more than one *o*, words such as *too* are accepted, but because, cooperation has only one *t*, *toot* is not acceptable. Words can be any length. The game proceeds as follows:

1. Students work alone to write words that fit the criteria (e.g., *a, at, pat, rat, cat, rant, in, tin, pin, print, too, per, open, pant, train, pain, rain, action, pact, part, pear, tear*).

2. Students then count the words they have created and write that number on the top of their paper.

3. Next, students work with a partner to create a combined list that contains the words on each person's list, minus duplicates (e.g., if both have *in* on their lists, it is counted once). In this step, perhaps some of their partner's words can inspire more words. These new words are added to each person's combined list.

4. Partners then count the number of words on this longer list and write the new number on the top of their paper, this time with a circle around the number.

Beware: This game is addictive, and students may want to continue playing even after the class has switched to another activity.

CHAPTER 8

Cooperative Learning and the United Nations' Sustainable Development Goals

In 2015, the United Nations proposed 17 Sustainable Development Goals (SDGs; United Nations, 2023). These goals include ending poverty and hunger; providing everyone with clean water, sanitation, and quality education; and protecting the environment. Though progress has been made toward achieving these goals, millions of people still die annually from the problems listed in the 17 SDGs. Additionally, the climate crisis is worsening, leading perhaps unstoppably to detrimental changes in our planet's ecosystems—changes from which the poor will suffer much more than the wealthy, although the wealthy are responsible for the release of much more greenhouse gas (Thunberg, 2022).

It is impossible to completely achieve any of the SDGs by 2030, the date targeted by the United Nations. However, we can celebrate small gains while we continue toward more complete attainment. To that end, education stakeholders should consider making the SDGs a major priority of education systems.

Cooperative Learning and the Sustainable Development Goals

How do the SDGs connect to cooperative learning (CL)? First, successful education prepares students to engage with the SDGs, and, as explained throughout this book, CL can be a key part of successful education. Second, the CL principle of *cooperation as a value* aims to expand the feeling of *positive interdependence* beyond the small group. This expansion can reach to the entire classroom, the entire school, and all the way to the entire world, including other species.

 REFLECTIVE BREAK

Most lists of CL principles do not include *cooperation as a value*. Is *cooperation as a value* an important principle? Is it practical, or is it too idealistic?

Dewey, as quoted in Chapter 5, highlighted that the key goal of education lies not in the advancement of individual students (e.g., earning a degree as a stepping stone for a prestigious and financially secure career), but instead in their contributions to the advancement of society generally. Similarly, Einstein is said to have urged people to increase their circles of compassion, meaning those other beings about whom we care (Popova, 2016).

In this chapter, we will briefly describe two CL techniques that might be useful when students work to achieve the SDGs at the same time as they boost their English proficiency. These techniques are Group Investigation (Sharan & Sharan, 1992) and Cooperative Debate (Johnson & Johnson, 1995).

Technique: Group Investigation

Group Investigation was designed to implement Dewey's ideas. In this technique, the class functions as a group of groups. The class chooses a topic, such as how to advance one of the SDGs, although Group Investigation can work with any topic. Next, each group develops a subtopic from the class's larger topic. An example could be that SDG5 (quality education) is the class topic, and one group could work on the subtopic of inclusion—for example, the inclusion of students from refugee families or of special needs students.

Next, groups discuss how they will go about investigating their subtopic and divide up the work. After group mates report what they learned, groups discuss again and perhaps investigate again. Then, groups plan a presentation to the entire class, including ideas for actions that can be taken individually and collectively, and rehearse their presentation to align with criteria decided by the class. Every student has a speaking part in this presentation.

Technique: Cooperative Debate

Many debates have arisen as to how to achieve the SDGs. Debates have long been used in education; however, the traditional debate format focuses on competition, not on *cooperation as a value*. Thus, Cooperative Debate, also known as Structured Academic Controversy or Creative Controversy, was developed with CL principles in mind. The steps are as follows, but please bear in mind that CL techniques can be modified.

First, the class chooses a debate topic. Students then form heterogeneous groups of four, divided into pairs. Each pair in the foursomes is given one side on the issue being debated; they cannot choose their position. An example of a debate topic under both SDG3 (good health and well-being) and SDG13 (climate action) would be "Should governments subsidize consumption of plant foods, such as vegetables, fruits, beans, and tubers?" Pair A could be assigned to argue in support of subsidization, and Pair B could be assigned to argue against. Next, pairs prepare to present their assigned view, and to facilitate both *individual accountability* and *equal opportunity to participate*, pairs rehearse their presentation to check if each partner speaks for approximately the same amount of time.

When the debate begins, each pair presents, while the other pair in the foursome takes notes and acts as timekeepers. Following the initial presentation of views, each group member rebuts one or more points made earlier by the other pair. Then, open discussion takes place, with everyone keeping to their assigned view on the topic.

For the second round of Cooperative Debate, pairs change sides and speak in favor of the view which they had previously opposed. In our food example, Pair A, who had favored subsidizing plant foods, now must speak against it, while Pair B is now in favor. This assigned shift of positions allows students to not just hear or read different perspectives; even more deeply, students must represent different positions.

The final step may be the key part of Cooperative Debate. Although students remain in their foursomes, they are on their own. They no longer have an assigned view. Rather, during three to five minutes of silent time, each student develops their own stance on the issue. That stance could be either of the two assigned views, or possibly a third view. For instance, a third stance on the issue of whether to subsidize consumption of plant food might be to help people grow their own food at home, even if they live in a flat. To complete the activity, the groups strive for consensus while they also practice using cooperative skills.

 REFLECTIVE BREAK

Could you see yourself using either Group Investigation or Cooperative Debate with your students? Why or why not?

To conclude this chapter, let's look at two concepts that link to cooperation as a value and the SDGs.

Abundance Not Scarcity

When we operate with a feeling of scarcity, we worry that we will not have enough, whether this means enough essentials in life, such as food, or enough nonessentials, such as opportunities to vacation in other countries. No amount is ever enough; we feel as though we always need more. If we have a feeling of scarcity, we may not want to help others who have less with money, time, or in other ways.

Contrasting with a feeling of scarcity is a feeling of abundance. When we operate with a feeling of abundance, we believe that we have enough and that in times of difficulty we can adjust. As Gandhi famously said, "The world has enough for everyone's need, but not everyone's greed." (Balch, 2013).

Freudenfreude Instead of Schadenfreude

Schadenfreude is a German word which means feeling happy when bad things happen to others, such as when a fellow student stands up in class to answer a teacher's question but answers incorrectly. On an international scale, an especially shameful example of schadenfreude might be feeling happy when famine occurs in a distant part of the world (SDG2, zero hunger).

Freudenfreude is the opposite of schadenfreude. When we feel *freudenfreude*, we are happy when good things happen to others. We celebrate their happiness. For instance, another student performs a dance in front of the school, and everyone is impressed by their talent. Extended to a global perspective, *freudenfreude* describes why we are happy when more children as well as people over 60 gain access to education (SDG4, quality education).

 REFLECTIVE BREAK

Do you sometimes have the aforementioned feeling of scarcity? What about *schadenfreude*? If so, do you try to overcome these feelings, and if so, how?

CHAPTER **9**

Cooperation Among Teachers

This final chapter in the book explains why and how teachers can cooperate with their peers, starting with why teachers might benefit from peer cooperation. Do any of these reasons make sense based on your experience?

1. As the saying goes, "Many hands make light the work." For instance, teachers can cooperate with each other to create and revise materials.

2. Just as students in cooperative groups have more power to influence class and school policies by working together, so too do teachers have more power collectively than when speaking or otherwise acting alone.

3. Each teacher has different experiences and perspectives. Bringing these experiences and perspectives together can be useful. For example, when a student is facing difficulties, teachers can work together to help that student.

4. Each teacher has different strengths and weaknesses. Teachers can help each other make weaknesses into strengths, such as in the common story of a tech-savvy teacher helping a less tech-proficient colleague improve their IT skills.

5. A Native American proverb states, "Happiness was born a twin—to experience joy, we must share it." Fellow teachers can share successes, as well as frustrations. It's great to have someone who "gets it" when we share minor victories, or even a small step toward a victory.

6. Perhaps the key benefit of teacher–teacher cooperation is that by tasting success via cooperation with their peers, teachers become more passionate about providing their students with opportunities to experience success with their own peers. Furthermore, teachers who cooperate with their peers have a more authentic voice when facilitating student–student cooperation.

Note that many of these advantages of teacher–teacher cooperation are at least partly social and affective, rather than only cognitive. Even though teachers spend many hours surrounded by students in classrooms, teaching can be a lonely job. Those hours with students are not the same as time spent with peers. In addition, teachers who become comfortable working cooperatively often begin to gather for nonacademic activities, such as birthday celebrations, eating together, and exercising together. Thus, cooperating with fellow teachers can boost teachers' mental health.

 REFLECTIVE BREAK

Have you experienced any of the advantages of teacher–teacher collaboration, either those mentioned in this section or others?

Now that we've seen the advantages that result when teachers work together, here are some ways to promote cooperation among teachers:

1. Teachers can learn or relearn cooperative learning (CL) techniques (and discuss possible modifications to them) when such techniques are modeled at staff and department meetings, as well as at professional development sessions.

2. When teachers form committees, just as in student groups, each member can have a role in order to promote the CL principle of positive interdependence (as discussed in Chapter 4).

3. CL principles, such as individual accountability and equal opportunity to participate (see Chapter 4), can be attended to in teacher groups using the same suggestions applicable to group activities for students.

4. Teachers can come together in unions or similar organizations to provide administrators, governments, and other stakeholders with teacher perspectives on various issues. Furthermore, teachers can network with colleagues at other schools, even in other countries, to share ideas and concerns.

5. Nurses sometimes meet in journal clubs to read and discuss articles and other materials relevant to their professional lives. Teachers can do something similar.

6. Teachers can collaborate on doable, classroom-sized research, such as action research, and eventually give conference presentations together.

7. Similarly, teachers can observe each other's teaching and provide positive feedback. An easy way to organize this is to videotape one another and view the videos together.

 REFLECTIVE BREAK

Have you tried any of these ways for teachers to cooperate or seen colleagues try them? If so, were any of them successful?

To conclude this chapter and this book, let us share again our enthusiasm for cooperation as a way of learning, a way of teaching, and an overall way of life. Individual achievements, as well as competition, have important places in life—but cooperation may well be the most important form of human activity. Yes, cooperation can be difficult, even after years of experience. Fortunately, the efforts made to overcome those difficulties are indeed worthwhile. As you make those efforts, we hope you find the contents of this book helpful. Please do share the book with others as one more form of cooperation.

References

Allport, G. W. (1954). *The nature of prejudice*. AddisonWesley.

Archambault, R. D. (Ed.). (1964). *John Dewey on education: Selected writings*. The Modern Library.

Aronson, E. (2023). *The jigsaw classroom*. http://www.jigsaw.org

Balch, O. (2013, January 28). The relevance of Gandhi in the capitalism debate. *The Guardian*. https://www.theguardian.com/sustainable-business/blog/relevance-gandhi-capitalism-debate-rajni-bakshi

Benson, P. (2011). *Teaching and researching autonomy* (2nd ed.). Pearson Education.

Dornyei, Z. (2020). *Innovations and challenges in language learning motivation*. Routledge.

Dweck, C. S. (2017). *Mindset: Changing the way you think to fulfill your potential* (Rev. ed.). Robinson.

Ellis, R. (2012). *Language teaching research and language pedagogy*. John Wiley & Sons.

Farrell, T. S. C., & Jacobs, G. M. (2020). *Essentials for successful language teaching* (2nd ed.). Bloomsbury.

Fushino, K. (2010). Causal relationships between communication confidence, beliefs about group work, and willingness to communicate in foreign language group work. *TESOL Quarterly, 44*(4), 700–724.

Gillies, R. M. (2019). Dialogic talk in the cooperative classroom. In R. M. Gillies (Ed.), *Promoting academic talk in schools: Global practices and perspectives* (pp. 144–160). Routledge. https://doi.org/10.4324/9780203728932-10

Helgesen, M. (2019). *English teaching and the science of happiness: Positive psychology communication activities for language learning*. ABAX.

Ivone, F. M., Jacobs, G. M., & Renandya, W. A. (2020). Far apart, yet close together: Cooperative learning in online education. *Studies in English Language and Education, 7*(2), 271–289. http://jurnal.unsyiah.ac.id/SiELE/article/view/17285/12678

Jacobs, G. M., Kimura, H., & Greliche, N. (2016). Incivility among group mates in English classes at a Japanese women's university. *TESL-EJ, 19*(4), 1–16. http://www.tesl-ej.org/pdf/ej76/a6.pdf

Jacobs, G. M., Lie, A., & Tamah, S. M. (2022). *Cooperative learning through a reflective lens.* Equinox.

Jacobs, G. M., & Power, M. A. (2016). Student centered learning: An approach to fostering democracy in schools. *Beyond Words, 4*(2), 79–87. http://journal.wima.ac.id/index.php/BW/article/view/884/pdf

Johnson, D. W., & Johnson, R. T. (1995). *Creative controversy: Intellectual challenge in the classroom* (3rd ed.). Interaction Book Company.

Johnson, D. W., & Johnson, R. T. (2009). An educational psychology success story: Social independence theory and cooperative learning. *Educational Researcher, 38*(5), 365–379.

Johnson, D. W., Johnson, R. T., & Holubec, E. J. (2021). Using cooperative learning in on-line classes. *The Cooperative Link, 35*(1), 1–3. http://www.co-operation.org/journal-articles

Leary, M. R. (1995). *Self-presentation: Impression management and interpersonal behavior.* Westview Press.

Little, D. (2022). Language learner autonomy: Rethinking language teaching. *Language Teaching, 55*(1), 64–73. https://doi.org/10.1017/S0261444820000488

Marrow, A. J. (1977). *The practical theorist: The life and work of Kurt Lewin.* Teachers College Press.

McCafferty, S., Jacobs, G., & Iddings, A. C. (Eds.). (2006). *Cooperative learning and second language teaching.* Cambridge University Press.

Ogle, D. M. (1986). K-W-L: A teaching model that develops active reading of expository text. *The Reading Teacher, 39*(6), 564–570. https://www.jstor.org/stable/20199156

Popova, M. (2016, November 28). *Einstein on widening our circles of compassion.* The Marginalian. https://www.themarginalian.org/2016/11/28/einstein-circles-of-compassion/

Rivers, W. (1976). *Speaking in many tongues: Essays in foreign language teaching* (2nd ed.). Newbury House.

Santosa, M. H., Ivone, F. M., Jacobs, G. M., & Flores, J. C. (2022). Student-to-student cooperation in virtual learning without breakout rooms. *Beyond Words, 10*(1), 70-82. http://jurnal.wima.ac.id/index.php/BW/article/view/3774

Seligman, M. E. (2011). *Flourish: A visionary new understanding of happiness and well-being.* Free Press.

Seligman, M. E. P., & Adler, A. (2019). Positive education. In J. F. Helliwell, R. Layard, & J. Sachs (Eds.), *Global happiness and wellbeing policy report 2019* (pp. 52–71). Global Council for Wellbeing and Happiness.

Sharan, Y., & Sharan, S. (1992). *Expanding cooperative learning through group investigation.* Teachers College Press.

Thunberg, G. (2022). *The climate book.* Random House.

Tokuhama-Espinosa, T. (2021). *Bringing the neuroscience of learning to online teaching.* Teachers College Press.

Tomasello, M. (2009). *Why we cooperate.* MIT Press.

United Nations. (2023). *17 goals.* https://sdgs.un.org/goals

Wolf, W., & Tomasello, M. (2020). Human children, but not great apes, become socially closer by sharing an experience in common ground. *Journal of Experimental Child Psychology, 199,* 104930. https://doi.org/10.1016/j.jecp.2020.104930

About the Authors

George M. Jacobs teaches in person and by distance in Singapore (where he has lived since 1993) and by distance in other countries, including Indonesia, Japan, Korea, Malaysia, the Philippines, and Thailand. His academic interests include student-centric pedagogies and bringing global issues into the language classroom. Among his recent publications are the book *Cooperative Learning Through a Reflective Lens*, with Anita Lie and Siti Mina Tamah (2022), published by Equinox and the article "Combining Extensive Reading While Listening with Cooperative Learning" in the *Journal of Applied Linguistics and Literature* with Kaoru Tsuda, Noriko Muramatsu, and Willy A. Renandya.

Harumi Kimura is a professor at Miyagi Gakuin Women's University in Sendai, Japan. Her doctoral research focused on second language (L2) listening anxiety, and her academic interests include L2 learner psychology and cooperative learning. She has recently contributed a chapter, "Listening and Affective Factors," to the *Routledge Handbook of Second Language Acquisition and Listening* (in press) with Xian Zhang. She regularly writes for the bulletin of the Japan Association for Language Teaching's Mind, Brain, and Education Special Interest Group, *MindBrained Think Tanks,* which spreads ideas about how to apply neuroscientific findings to L2 teaching and learning.

About the Series Editor

Thomas S. C. Farrell, PhD, is a professor at Brock University, Canada. His professional interests include reflective practice and second language teacher education and development. He has published widely in these areas. His work can be found at www.reflectiveinquiry.ca.